UNDERSTANDING GESTALT PLAY THERAPY

Mastering The Art Of Gestalt Play Practices To Navigating Targeted Interventions, Implementing Effective Strategies, Targeted Techniques, Key Principles

DR. KARSON BRYAN

Copyright © 2023, Dr. Karson Bryan

DISCLAIMER

This book's content is meant to be used solely for general informative purposes. Despite having taken every precaution to guarantee the content's accuracy, the author disclaims all duty and responsibility for any errors or omissions. It is recommended that readers exercise caution and, if needed, seek expert guidance. Any and all liability for losses, damages, or other outcomes arising from the use of the material included in this book is disclaimed by the author and publisher. All referenced product names and trademarks are the property of their respective owners and are merely cited for identification. Any likeness to real people or things is entirely accidental. Since it is a work of fiction, this book should not be used as a substitute for professional, legal, or medical advice. It is advised that readers seek advice on particular issues from qualified experts."

Please make sure that this disclaimer is modified to fit the particular requirements and subject matter of your book. Seeking advice from a legal expert is also a smart option if you have any questions or require a more thorough disclaimer for your specific book.

TABLE OF CONTENTS

CHAPTER ONE

GESTALT PLAY THERAPY

INTRODUCTION

KNOWING THE FUNDAMENTALS OF GESTALT PLAY THERAPY

Gestalt Play Therapy is a therapeutic technique that employs play as a healing and self-discovery tool while incorporating the ideas of Gestalt therapy. With the help of this cutting-edge approach, people especially kids can explore and comprehend their feelings, ideas, and experiences in a fun and engaging way. We will explore the idea of Gestalt Play Therapy, its historical background, important players, and the important role play plays in the therapeutic process in this introduction.

MEANING OF GESTALT PLAY THERAPY

Gestalt therapy, which was established in the 1940s by Fritz Perls, Laura Perls, and Paul

Goodman, is the foundation for the integrated therapeutic method known as Gestalt play therapy. This method places a strong emphasis on the value of the "here and now" experience by emphasizing the present, accountability, and self-awareness. These ideas are modified in the context of play therapy to meet the requirements of kids and adults who might find it difficult to express themselves in regular talk therapy.

The idea that people are inherently motivated to regulate themselves and grow is one of the main tenets of Gestalt play therapy. The facilitator, who is also the therapist, provides a secure and encouraging space for the client to engage in a variety of imaginative and lighthearted activities that allow them to explore their inner world. The use of drama, music, art, and other expressive mediums may be involved in this. Clients can acquire insight into their emotions, work through unsolved difficulties, and externalize their thoughts and feelings through these activities.

HISTORICAL EVOLUTION AND PRINCIPAL PLAYERS

Gestalt play therapy has its origins in the work of Fritz and Laura Perls, two of the pioneers of Gestalt therapy. By highlighting the significance of holistic awareness and the integration of the mind, body, and emotions, they established the groundwork for the Gestalt concepts. These ideas have been modified over time by researchers and therapists to meet the special requirements of kids and adults who face a range of emotional and psychological difficulties.

Prominent individuals like Violet Oaklander and Gary Yontef were instrumental in the development of Gestalt play therapy during the 20th century. Particularly Violet Oaklander is recognized by many as having played a significant role in the creation of this methodology. She made a substantial contribution to our knowledge of children's emotional development and therapeutic needs by fusing Gestalt ideas with play therapy approaches. Her contributions to the field of child treatment have had a long-lasting effect.

PLAY IS ESSENTIAL IN THERAPY

A basic and universal form of self-expression, learning, and experience interpretation, play is used by all humans. It is a vital tool in therapy because it acts as a language that is beyond words, particularly when working with youngsters or those who might find it difficult to express their thoughts and feelings orally. Play becomes the language of expression in Gestalt play therapy, enabling clients to interact and explore their inner world in a fun and safe way.

Play serves as a link between the self's conscious and unconscious selves. Clients can access deeper emotions, memories, and inner conflicts through creative and symbolic play activities that may be challenging to access through regular discourse. Through the exploration of one's inner landscape, the development of new coping mechanisms, and self-awareness, this therapy method eventually fosters growth and healing.

Gestalt Play Therapy combines the therapeutic benefits of play with the holistic and cutting-edge ideas of Gestalt therapy. This therapy approach respects the value of the present moment while providing people, especially kids, with an imaginative and stimulating means of connecting with their feelings and experiences. We will examine the tenets, methods, and uses of this approach as we dig further, illuminating the significant influence it may have on the healing process.

CHAPTER TWO

THE BASIS OF PLAY THERAPY IN GESTALT

The theoretical underpinnings of The Foundations of Gestalt Play Therapy blend the therapeutic advantages of play with the tenets of Gestalt psychology. This method offers a comprehensive and hands-on approach to treating children's emotional and psychological problems. Gestalt play therapy's essential theoretical tenets can be examined via an examination of its relationship to Gestalt psychology, the core ideas it embraces, and the way play and Gestalt principles are seamlessly combined.

GESTALT PSYCHOLOGY AND ITS INFLUENCE

The early 20th-century school of thinking known as Gestalt psychology is the source of Gestalt Play Therapy. Derived from the German word meaning "form" or "shape," the term "Gestalt" highlights the notion that the totality of things is greater than the sum of its parts. From this vantage point, human experience and perception are seen as integrated wholes rather than as a disparate set of parts. This translates into a focus on the patient's consciousness, the present, and their interactions with the surroundings in therapy.

IMPORTANT THEORETICAL IDEAS:

The basis of Gestalt play therapy is comprised of several important theoretical ideas. First and foremost, the idea of "here and now" is crucial. Children who can fully engage in the present moment might establish a stronger connection with their emotions, ideas, and sensory experiences, according to therapists. Children can develop a greater understanding of themselves through therapy, which places a strong emphasis on the value of self-awareness and self-acceptance.

"The cycle of awareness," which entails people going through different stages of awareness as they interact with their surroundings and experiences, including contact, withdrawal, and absorption, is another important idea. Children are led through this cycle in therapy, providing a secure and encouraging setting for them to investigate their emotions and perceptions.

Furthermore, Gestalt Play Therapy emphasizes the value of individual accountability. It teaches kids to accept responsibility for their thoughts, feelings, and deeds, which might enable them to transform their lives for the better. Children can learn how their emotions and behaviors are related through interaction and play that is supervised, which promotes personal development.

PLAY AND GESTALT PRINCIPLES

Gestalt Play Therapy combines the therapeutic benefits of play with the tenets of Gestalt psychology in a seamless manner. Children express themselves naturally via play, which gives them a nonverbal way to share their ideas, feelings, and experiences. Children can express themselves more freely and use their imaginations and creativity to explore their inner worlds when play is included in the therapy process.

Play and Gestalt ideas can be integrated through a variety of methods, including art therapy, role-playing, storytelling, and the use of objects and symbols. With the help of these techniques, kids can learn about their problems, externalize their internal conflicts, and resolve them in a context that is encouraging and judgment-free. As a guide, the therapist supports the child's investigation and assists them in drawing links between their play experiences and emotional health.

CHAPTER THREE

GESTALT PLAY THERAPY'S HEALING PARTNERSHIP

THE FUNCTION OF THE THERAPIST IN GESTALT PLAY THERAPY

The therapist is essential to the therapeutic process and the child's development as an emotionally mature child. This method, in contrast to conventional talk therapy, emphasizes play and creative expression as the main channels for self-expression and communication. To provide a supportive and stimulating atmosphere where the kid can explore their emotions and worries, the therapist adopts a variety of roles.

The facilitator position is one of the therapist's main responsibilities. Through play exercises, the therapist supports the child in expressing their feelings and experiences creatively and symbolically. Because this facilitation is non-directive, the kid is free to take the lead while the therapist watches, considers, and offers assistance as required. Establishing a genuine therapeutic relationship with a kid requires the therapist to be attuned to their needs, feelings, and behaviors.

In addition, the therapist helps the kids make meaning of their feelings and experiences by interpreting what they do in play. The therapist can spot themes and patterns in the child's play that might reveal underlying problems or conflicts through their interactions and observations. The child's individuality and self-discovery are respected during this delicate and non-intrusive interpretation process.

DEVELOPING TRUST AND RAPPORT

In Gestalt Play Therapy, developing trust and rapport is a critical component of the therapeutic alliance. For the child to feel comfortable expressing themselves, the therapist must provide a supportive and safe environment. This entails creating a solid foundation of connection and trust so that the child feels comfortable opening up and participating in the therapeutic process.

The therapist's constant presence, empathy, and sincere concern foster trust. For the child to feel valued and respected, the therapist must communicate acceptance, tenderness, and unconditional positive regard. To make sure the child is aware of the boundaries and expectations within the therapeutic relationship, the therapist should also be open and honest about the therapy process as well as the confidentiality guidelines.

Active listening and being aware of the wants and feelings of the child help to establish rapport. To make the child feel heard and understood, the therapist closely observes the youngster's nonverbal signs as well as verbal ones. A stronger bond and a feeling of real care are fostered by the therapist's sympathetic response to the child's signs and feelings.

ESTABLISHING A SAFE PLAY ENVIRONMENT

In Gestalt Play Therapy, the establishment of a safe play environment is essential because it provides a safe area for children to freely explore and express their feelings and experiences. The physical, psychological, and emotional components of the therapeutic environment are all included in safety.

In terms of furniture, the therapist makes sure the playroom has a range of developmentally appropriate toys and supplies to promote artistic expression. The actual area should be safe, cozy, and conducive to children's development to foster a sense of security.

In terms of emotions, the therapist creates a welcoming and nonjudgmental environment where the kids can express themselves without worrying about being rejected or criticized.

The youngster receives validation and respect from the therapist for their experiences and feelings. The youngster can take chances and explore challenging emotions in a safe environment because of this emotional safety.

Psychologically, the therapist upholds boundaries and secrecy, guaranteeing that the child's privacy is safeguarded and that they can rely on the confidentiality of the information they reveal during therapy. The youngster must understand that the therapeutic space is a safe place where they can be who they are without fear of negative consequences.

In brief, the therapist's functions in Gestalt Play Therapy include facilitation, interpretation, and compassionate guidance. Establishing a therapeutic relationship requires developing rapport and trust, and the therapist must provide a secure play setting that encourages emotional expression and investigation.

By using these ideas, kids can take part in meaningful therapy work and learn more about their feelings and experiences, which promotes personal development and healing.

CHAPTER FOUR

USING PLAY AS A HEALING TOOL

THE INFLUENCE OF PLAY

Psychologists and counselors have long acknowledged the therapeutic benefits of play. It is a normal and crucial part of human growth, and people of all ages can benefit from it therapeutically. Play can encourage self-expression, stimulate creativity, and aid in healing in a fun and non-threatening way. Play is a useful tool in many therapeutic approaches, including Gestalt therapy, since it enables people to connect with their inner selves, explore emotions, and build problem-solving abilities.

Play is a tool used in therapy to help clients communicate with one another, their therapist, and their surroundings. It establishes a secure environment in which patients can explore themselves, develop a relationship with their therapist, and deal with underlying emotional problems. Clients can acquire insight into their ideas, feelings, and actions by using play as a tool to externalize and resolve internal issues. Play has a transforming potential that is especially beneficial for children, but adults can also benefit from this therapeutic method.

DIFFERENT PLAY FORMS IN GESTALT THERAPY

Gestalt therapy is a holistic, experiential approach to counseling that embraces play as a way to deepen self-awareness and explore the present moment. Gestalt therapy frequently uses a variety of play techniques, each with a specific function:

1. Play that allows customers to express themselves creatively through art, music, dance, or theater is known as expressive play. When words are inadequate to accurately describe a client's inner world, expressive play offers a platform for them to express their emotions and experiences nonverbally.

2. Symbolic Play: This type of play enables clients to portray their connections, feelings, and thoughts with objects or symbols. To investigate and make meaning of their experiences, clients may utilize drawings, figurines, or other symbolic objects. Play like this can provide clients insight into their inner conflicts and wants and help them establish a connection with their subconscious.

3. Role-playing: In Gestalt therapy, role-playing is a potent tool that helps clients examines many facets of themselves and their points of view. It is possible for clients to play multiple roles and have conversations with different facets of themselves. This method can assist clients in integrating contradictory facets of themselves and uncovering underlying conflicts.

4. Body-Centered Play: This kind of play focuses on the emotions and feelings of the body. It is suggested that clients become more aware of their bodily sensations, such as tension, posture, and gestures. Clients can learn more about their

emotional states and behavioral patterns by developing a greater awareness of their bodies.

PLAY WITH SYMBOLISM AND METAPHOR

Within the paradigm of Gestalt therapy, play is used therapeutically with a great deal of symbolism and metaphor. Clients frequently use metaphors and symbols to express their feelings and inner experiences. The conscious and unconscious facets of the self can be connected using these symbols.

Clients may use play to symbolically symbolize disputes, concerns, or unresolved issues. A client might, for instance, use a picture to represent their anxiousness or a group of figurines to represent their family relationships. These symbols provide a springboard for introspection and self-revelation.

Conversely, metaphor enables clients to subtly communicate their emotions and ideas. Rather than addressing a specific issue head-on, clients may use metaphors to explain their experiences. A client might say, "I feel like I'm stuck in a dark tunnel with no way out," for example, which alludes to their sense of helplessness or captivity. Gestalt therapists are educated to assist clients in dissecting these symbols and metaphors to reveal their deeper meanings and relationships to the client's current circumstances.

Within the framework of Gestalt therapy, play is a potent and adaptable therapeutic technique that may be used to foster self-awareness, personal development, and healing. Through the application of many play techniques, such as expressive, symbolic, role-playing, and body-centered play, clients can participate in an artistic and hands-on process that facilitates their exploration of their inner selves.

Play that incorporates symbolism and metaphor improves the therapy process by assisting clients in connecting with their subconscious and gaining a deeper understanding of their feelings and experiences. The capacity of play to assist people in discovering their inner resources and transforming their lives in a significant way is ultimately what gives it its power in Gestalt therapy.

CHAPTER FIVE

GESTALT PLAY THERAPY METHODS AND STRATEGIES

THE PLAYFUL GESTALT CYCLE OF EXPERIENCE

The core idea of Gestalt Play Therapy techniques and methods is the Gestalt Cycle of Experience, a dynamic process that directs the client's or child's therapeutic journey. The five fundamental stages of this cycle are Assimilation, Awareness, Contact, Withdrawal, and Closure. In the context of play therapy, each of these stages is essential for fostering self-awareness, personal development, and emotional healing.

BEING AWARE

In play therapy, awareness is the first phase in the Gestalt Cycle of Experience. It has to do with the client's or child's ability to become aware of their feelings, ideas, and physical sensations in the here and now. This stage of play therapy is supported by the use of toys, sand, art, and other creative and expressive materials. By helping the kid to investigate their experiences in the present moment, the therapist aids in the child's development of self-awareness. The youngster starts the process of self-discovery by gaining insight into their emotional landscape and becoming aware of their inner world.

REACH OUT

After the awareness phase, contact focuses on the client's or child's capacity to interact with others and their immediate surroundings. Building a relationship with the therapist and the play therapy procedure itself is the focus of this phase. A secure and accepting atmosphere is created by the therapist, who serves as a sympathetic and encouraging figure, allowing the kids to freely express themselves.

The youngster can use play to explore their relationships with people, their feelings, and their surroundings.

RETRACTION

The subsequent stage of the cycle is called withdrawal, during which the child momentarily stops participating in the therapeutic process. It is critical to recognize that the child's withdrawal is a normal and crucial aspect of the cycle, giving them time to gather themselves and think back on their experiences. The therapist honors the child's demand for privacy, independence, or space during this stage. The youngster frequently gains awareness of their boundaries and self-control during this stage.

INTEGRATION

The process by which the child or client incorporates their newly acquired knowledge, experiences, and insights into their self-concept and coping mechanisms is known as assimilation. They come to terms with their emotions and experiences throughout this stage, giving their emotional world context and significance. To aid with this process, the therapist offers reflection opportunities and encourages the child to share their ideas and emotions on the events that have occurred during play therapy sessions.

FINALITY

In play therapy, closure denotes the end of the Gestalt Cycle of Experience. It entails the child or client consolidating their learning and growth and reflecting on their entire therapy experience. To assist the child in celebrating their development, the therapist acknowledges the good changes, realizations, and individual accomplishments that have occurred during therapy. Closure might also involve talking about long-term objectives or ways to keep up the therapeutic gains.

The Gestalt Cycle of Experience serves as a fundamental framework in play therapy, directing the therapeutic process. From Awareness to Closure, every stage advances the child's emotional development, self-awareness, and healing. The therapist can assist the child in exploring and integrating their experiences by utilizing a variety of creative strategies and tactics, which will ultimately result in a more emotionally resilient and healthy adult. This method, which has its roots in Gestalt therapy, places a strong emphasis on the value of being in the moment, developing real connections, and encouraging self-acceptance and personal integration.

CHAPTER SIX

PLAY THERAPY ACTIVITIES FOR GESTALT

THE METHOD OF THE EMPTY CHAIR

In Gestalt Play Therapy, the Empty Chair Technique is a potent and popular therapeutic activity. It's a technique that helps people especially kids to externalize their feelings, ideas, and disputes by having them imagine that something or someone is seated in an empty chair. The Gestalt psychology idea of "unfinished business," which refers to unresolved feelings or problems with oneself or others, is the foundation of this technique. Clients can use the empty chair to project their sentiments into a fictional person or even a part of themselves and have a conversation that helps them understand their thoughts, problems, and possible solutions. This method encourages self-expression and self-awareness, enabling clients to face their inner demons in a therapeutic setting that is secure and encouraging.

CREATIVE EXPRESSION AND THE ARTS

Creating Art and Expressing Oneself are essential elements of Gestalt Play Therapy. Drawing, painting, sculpting, and other artistic mediums are used to support adults and children in exploring their feelings and ideas. This method acknowledges the importance of creativity as a tool for self-expression and communication. Clients can access deeper psychological layers and get past verbal obstacles through the medium of art. In therapy, the use of art and creative expression helps clients process their feelings and experiences, which promotes self-awareness and personal development.

PLAYING ROLES AND DRAMA

Gestalt play therapy is based on role-play and drama. These methods give clients children in particular the ability to adopt new personas, situations, and viewpoints. People can learn more about their own and other people's actions by role-playing. Through enacting particular scenarios or disputes, individuals can investigate different approaches to reacting and resolving issues. By having clients put themselves in other people's shoes through role-playing and drama, clients can develop empathy and gain a greater knowledge of interpersonal dynamics and different points of view. Using an experienced approach, clients can enhance their social and communication skills and learn new coping mechanisms.

SAND TRAY INTERVENTION

Another useful instrument in Gestalt Play Therapy is Sand Tray Therapy. With this technique, clients construct scenes, symbols, and narratives that reflect their inner world and experiences using a tray full of sand and a range of little objects and figurines. Clients can access and process unconscious ideas and emotions by placing these objects in the sand. To help the client develop an understanding of their own story and reveal buried conflicts and desires, the therapist collaborates with them to examine the meaning of these creations. Sand tray therapy can be very helpful for people who find it difficult to express their emotions vocally because it provides a nonverbal, symbolic avenue for self-expression.

DREAMING IN ACTION

Dream Work in Play is a method that incorporates dream interpretation into the healing process. Dreams are thought to be a rich source of symbolic information that might reveal a person's unconscious thoughts and emotional difficulties. Within the therapy setting, clients are encouraged to discuss and investigate their dreams in Gestalt Play Therapy.

In this investigation, the symbols, feelings, and stories that are present in the dream are discussed, and their potential connections to the client's waking life are taken into account. The objective is to assist clients in becoming more self-aware, reaching out to the deeper levels of their psyche, and resolving any conflicts or unresolved issues that may be coming up in their dreams. Dream work in play therapy provides chances for personal development and healing as well as a comprehensive awareness of the client's inner world.

To help people, especially children, access their inner thoughts, feelings, and conflicts, Gestalt Play Therapy uses a range of techniques and procedures, including the Empty Chair Technique, Art and Creative Expression, Role Play and Drama, Sand Tray Therapy, and Dream work in Play. These therapy methods encourage clients to participate in creative and experiential processes, which eventually promote healing and well-being and aid in the development of self-awareness, self-expression, and personal growth.

Because each of these methods is customized to the particular requirements and preferences of the client, Gestalt Play Therapy is a flexible and successful therapeutic strategy.

CHAPTER SEVEN

DEALING WITH PARTICULAR POPULATIONS

GESTPLAY THERAPY AND CHILDREN

Working with children who may be experiencing a range of emotional and behavioral challenges can be done creatively and very successfully using Gestalt Play Therapy. By encouraging children to express themselves through play, this therapy approach enables them to interact non-directly and symbolically with their ideas, feelings, and experiences. Through this method, children can explore their thoughts, feelings, and interpersonal interactions in a safe and compassionate atmosphere created by the therapist.

Children are encouraged to express themselves via art in a variety of ways during Gestalt Play Therapy sessions, including painting, drawing, storytelling, and interactive games. This method works especially well with kids since it follows their innate desire to play and explore their surroundings. Children can enhance their problem-solving abilities, obtain a better understanding of their emotions, and grow in self-awareness through creative and imaginative activities.

TEENS AND GESTALT PLAY THERAPY

Adolescents and Gestalt Play Therapy can also be used together well. Teens frequently experience particular difficulties with identity, relationships, and personal development; this therapeutic method offers a framework that is both structured and adaptable to meet their requirements. Adolescents may be more likely to explore their ideas and feelings verbally in addition to through creative pursuits like theater, art, or sand tray treatment.

The goals of Gestalt play therapy for teenagers are to support their growth in self-acceptance, self-awareness, and sense of responsibility. It helps children develop a better awareness of their emotional reactions and empowers them to accept responsibility for their decisions and behaviors. Through this therapy, adolescents can gain an understanding of their behavior patterns, develop better communication skills, and resolve concerns about their self-worth, connections with peers, and family dynamics.

GESTALT PLAY THERAPY AND ADULTS

While it is typically used with children and teenagers, adults can also benefit from its adaptations. This method can be helpful for adults dealing with a range of emotional difficulties, including depression, anxiety, trauma, and relationship problems. Gestalt therapy's basic ideas self-awareness and the present moment remain applicable even though adults may employ play therapy methods differently than children.

Gestalt play therapy for adults may use dance, art, or other creative techniques that support self-expression. Adults can identify patterns of behavior and thought, obtain a better knowledge of their emotions, and strive toward personal development and healing via the guided examination of their thoughts and experiences. This method promotes empowerment, self-acceptance, and the capacity for real living.

FAMILIES AND COUPLES IN PLAY THERAPY

Using play therapy in conjunction with standard talk therapy can be very beneficial in family and couples therapy. In a family or couple setting, gestalt play therapy facilitates the examination of intricate relationship dynamics and communication styles. It offers a secure environment where family members or couples may communicate their emotions, work out disagreements, and strengthen their bonds.

To deal with problems like mixed family dynamics, sibling rivalry, and parenting obstacles, families can become creative and play games together.

Play therapy practices are a useful tool for couples to improve intimacy, resolve issues, and forge stronger emotional relationships. Gestalt play therapy's non-directive approach encourages patients to accept their feelings, stay in the present, and develop more constructive interpersonal relationships. This method can be particularly useful when verbal communication is not enough to resolve deeply ingrained problems in families and relationships.

CHAPTER EIGHT

RESOLVING EMOTIONAL INJURIES AND TRAUMA

GESTALT PLAY THERAPY WITH A TRAUMA LENS

Trauma-informed Gestalt Play Therapy is a novel and successful method for helping adults and children heal from emotional trauma and scars. This therapeutic approach blends aspects of play therapy and Gestalt therapy to offer a secure and supportive setting for people to process and heal from traumatic events.

Gestalt treatment emphasizes the present moment and helps patients become more conscious of their ideas, feelings, and sensations. This strategy becomes an effective tool for treating and healing trauma when combined with play therapy, which is especially helpful for kids and others who might have trouble expressing themselves verbally.

Therapists who use Trauma-Informed Gestalt Play Therapy provide a safe, accepting environment for their patients to use a variety of expressive and creative methods to examine their traumatic experiences. People naturally make sense of their experiences and emotions through play, especially young toddlers who might not be able to express their sentiments verbally. Clients can process and relive their trauma in a safe and regulated setting through play.

This therapeutic approach acknowledges that a person's relationships, sense of self, and general well-being can all be significantly impacted by trauma. Therapists can assist clients in making a comprehensive connection with their emotions and experiences by incorporating Gestalt ideas. Through this process, people can better understand how trauma has affected their lives and how to take steps to heal and recover.

For Trauma-Informed Gestalt Play Therapy, developing a solid therapeutic alliance between the therapist and the client is essential. To heal from trauma, a client must first build a stable bond with their therapist. Only then can they feel comfortable enough to address their experience.

CASE STUDIES IN THE HEALING OF TRAUMA

Case studies in the field of trauma healing offer priceless insights into the efficacy of different therapeutic modalities, such as trauma-informed Gestalt play therapy. These real-life case studies provide hope and inspiration for therapists and clients alike by demonstrating how people have effectively navigated the process of recovering from trauma.

A youngster who has gone through a traumatic incident, like abuse or the death of a loved one, maybe the subject of one of these case studies. The child is encouraged to express their feelings and thoughts about the trauma through a variety of creative methods, including role-playing, storytelling, and sketching, through Trauma-Informed Gestalt Play Therapy. The child gradually lessens the emotional distress linked to the trauma over several sessions as they start to analyze and integrate their experiences.

An adult automobile accident survivor who acquired post-traumatic stress disorder (PTSD) might be the focus of another case study. This person uses creative strategies and experiential exercises in Trauma-Informed Gestalt Play Therapy to deal with overwhelming anxiety and flashbacks related to the accident. They learn to reframe their perceptions of the traumatic incident by engaging with a therapist who employs this technique, which eventually lessens the intensity of their PTSD symptoms.

The significance of customized treatment strategies is also emphasized by these case studies. Since every person's experience with trauma is different, what works for one person might not work for another.

CHAPTER NINE

GESTALT PLAY THERAPY IN EDUCATIONAL ENVIRONMENTS AND SCHOOLS

PLAY THERAPY IN EDUCATIONAL SETTINGS

Play therapy is a potent therapeutic strategy that can be used to assist children's emotional and psychological well-being in educational environments such as schools. Gestalt play therapy is one particular approach in the field of play therapy that emphasizes an individual's complete development. This method is effective in meeting students' emotional needs because it uses play as a vehicle for self-expression, healing, and self-discovery. Schools can foster a more welcoming and encouraging environment for their students by incorporating Gestalt Play Therapy into their classrooms.

In schools, gestalt play therapy involves giving kids a controlled, secure environment in which to play in a variety of ways. This approach's central tenet is that kids can actively process their emotions and psychological problems via play and creative expression. The therapist acts as a guide, assisting the kids in self-exploration and aiding in the understanding of their ideas and feelings. Typically, the therapist is a licensed play therapist or school counselor. Play sessions facilitate the development of therapeutic relationships that enable students to address a variety of challenges, including anxiety, trauma, behavioral problems, and self-esteem issues.

The understanding that a student's capacity to learn and achieve academic success is intimately linked to their emotional and psychological well-being is the driving force behind the decision to implement Gestalt Play Therapy in schools. Better academic results can be achieved by schools addressing the emotional components of a child's life. Students can process their emotions and experiences through play therapy, especially when using the Gestalt approach, which helps to lower emotional barriers that could impede their cognitive growth. This ultimately helps to establish a more productive and inclusive learning environment.

GESTALT PLAY AS A SUPPORT FOR EDUCATIONAL GOALS

Numerous significant educational objectives are supported and aligned with Gestalt Play Therapy in educational contexts. This method, which emphasizes the whole growth of the student, can support the development of social skills, emotional intelligence, and self-awareness—all of which are critical components of success in both academic and personal endeavors. Together, therapists and educators can use play therapy's ability to enhance the educational process and accomplish the following goals:

1. Better Emotional Regulation: Students who get Gestalt play therapy are given the skills necessary to comprehend and control their emotions. Their ability to focus and participate in the learning process is subsequently improved. Students can do better academically by managing pressures and distractions more effectively by tackling emotional control.

2. Enhanced Self-Esteem and Confidence: Students can explore and express their emotions, gain self-assurance, and cultivate a good self-image through play therapy sessions. Increased motivation, a more upbeat attitude toward learning, and a readiness to take on scholastic challenges can all be attributed to higher self-esteem.

3. Improved Communication Skills: Students are encouraged to express their ideas and feelings in a non-verbal, non-threatening way through Gestalt Play Therapy. To successfully collaborate on group assignments, resolve problems, and

actively participate in class discussions, one must develop strong communication skills.

4. Taking Care of Behavioral Issues: A lot of kids may experience behavioral problems that hinder their ability to learn. To promote a more upbeat and cooperative attitude in the classroom, Gestalt play therapy can assist in identifying and addressing the underlying emotional roots of these actions.

5. Fostering Resilience: Students who participate in therapeutic play activities gain resilience and the ability to adjust to adversity. Their ability to bounce back from losses, overcome challenges, and persevere in their academic pursuits is a result of their resilience.

Gestalt play therapy is an effective strategy for meeting children's emotional and psychological needs in learning environments like classrooms. It supports emotional control, self-worth, good communication, and resilience all of which are in line with educational objectives. Schools may foster a more welcoming and encouraging environment that not only improves students' mental health but also opens doors for greater academic achievement and personal development by incorporating this therapeutic approach.

CHAPTER TEN

GESTALT PLAY THERAPY INCORPORATED INTO CLINICAL PRACTICE

EVALUATION AND TREATMENT STRATEGY DEVELOPMENT

Integrating Gestalt Play Therapy into clinical practice requires careful consideration of both assessment and treatment strategy development. Gestalt Play Therapy offers a special method for comprehending and meeting the emotional and psychological needs of children by fusing the ideas of Gestalt therapy with the medium of play. In this case, the evaluation method includes close observation of the child's play activities and interactions in addition to standard diagnostic techniques. Therapists can learn a great deal about the child's inner world, emotional difficulties, and any underlying problems that might be hurting their well-being by making this observation.

The goal of Gestalt play therapy is to meet children where they are in their developmental process. This means that each child's requirements, preferences, and level of preparation should be taken into account while determining their course of therapy. As play is thought of as children's language, therapists must provide a secure and supportive atmosphere where kids can express themselves via play. Therapists collaborate with the child throughout the treatment planning process, offering innovative approaches to support them in exploring their emotions, ideas, and experiences. Therapy goals are set, and interventions are created to support children in reaching these goals while promoting their emotional development and self-awareness.

ETHICAL CONSIDERATIONS

It is crucial to take ethics into account when incorporating Gestalt play therapy into clinical practice. To protect the well-being, privacy, and safety of the children and families they work with, therapists are required to abide by the ethical standards that are outlined in the field. This method is based on fundamental ethical concepts, including beneficence, non-malfeasance, and autonomy.

As in any therapy context, confidentiality is a basic ethical element in Gestalt Play Therapy. Therapists must set up unambiguous boundaries and precautions to ensure the privacy of the child and their family. In addition, the kid and their caretakers need to be educated about the therapy process and given their agreement. Through open communication and well-informed decision-making, the child's autonomy is maintained and they are allowed to actively engage in their therapeutic journey.

PROFESSIONAL DEVELOPMENT AND SUPERVISION

Including Gestalt Play Therapy in therapeutic practice requires both continuous professional development and supervision. This method involves regular supervision so that therapists can evaluate their work, get new perspectives, and get advice on challenging cases. Therapists can talk about their experiences, difficulties, and triumphs in supervision and get helpful criticism and encouragement from seasoned supervisors.

Gestalt Play Therapy therapists are committed to continuous professional growth. To advance their careers, they need to learn new skills constantly and remain current on the most recent findings and methods in the industry. Therapy professionals can enhance their therapeutic skills and broaden their knowledge by attending conferences, workshops, and advanced training programs. By committing to their professional development, therapists may be sure that the children and families they work with receive the finest treatment available.

Incorporating Gestalt play therapy into clinical practice necessitates a thorough approach to evaluation and treatment planning, a dedication to professional growth and supervision, and a commitment to ethical issues. In addition to assisting therapists in giving children effective care, these fundamental ideas guarantee that the therapeutic process is carried out in an ethical, responsible, and ever-improving manner.

www.ingramcontent.com/pod-product-compliance
Lightning Source LLC
Chambersburg PA
CBHW060807260726
48660CB00002B/826